W9-AHJ-668

APR 2012

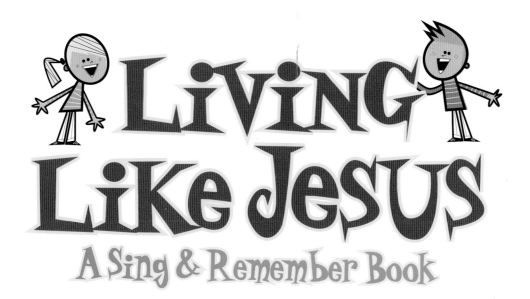

Living Like Jesus
A Sing & Remember Book

Created by
Stephen Elkins

Illustrations by
David Semple

INTEGRITY®
PUBLISHERS
family
Nashville

About the Author: S T E P H E N E L K I N S is one of America's foremost children's writers whose work has sold over 5 million children's books and CD's. He has received numerous awards including a nomination for the prestigious GRAMMY AWARD. Stephen has over 300 books, audio productions and DVD's to his credit including *The Memory Bible, The LullaBible* and *The Word & Song Bible.* Owner of Wonder Workshop, which is reported to be the 5th largest independent children's production company in the world (*BillBoard Magazine*), his books and children's Bibles remain at the top of the Best-Sellers list, as well as The Wonder Kids Choir recordings which maintained over 100 consecutive weeks on *BillBoard's* Top Kid Audio Chart in 2003. Stephen's workshops on music and Scripture Memory for Children continue to be very successful. Stephen lives in Nashville with his wife Cindy and their three children.

L I V I N G L I K E J E S U S
A Sing & Remember Book

Stories and songs written by Stephen Elkins.

Published by Integrity Publishers, a division of Integrity Media, Inc., 5250 Virginia Way, Suite 110, Brentwood, TN 37027.

www.integritypublishers.com

I N T E G R I T Y P U B L I S H E R S , I N C .
H E L P I N G P E O P L E W O R L D W I D E E X P E R I E N C E *the* M A N I F E S T P R E S E N C E *of* G O D

Illustrated by David Semple

Cover and interior design: Russ McIntosh, Mark Mickel, Brand Navigation, LLC—www.brandnavigation.com

Special thanks to: The Wonder Kids Choir: Emily Elkins, Laurie Harper, Audrey Hollifield, Amy Lawrence, Lindsey McAdams, Amy McPeak, and Allie Smith.

Engineer: Randy Moore

Arrangements: John DeVries

Library of Congress Cataloging-in-Publication Data
ISBN: 1-59145-431-X

Printed in China

06 07 08 09 RRD 9 8 7 6 5 4 3 2 1

TABLE OF CONTENTS

To Live like Jesus... Praise GOD

Let everything that has breath praise the LORD.

Psalm 150:6

THINKIN' 2day

You have breath, right?

What do you use it for? Dogs can use their breath to bark. Cats can use their breath to meow. Birds can sing, and lions can roar. But only people can use their breath to speak and sing. You can use words to express your thoughts. But most of all, you should use your breath to praise the Lord!

1

Noah and the Flood

(Around 2344 B.C.)

Noah once breathed in the funny smell of thousands of animals all packed into one boat. But he spoke out words of praise to God, because he loved the Lord! God told Noah to build an ark and gather all the animals together, two of every kind. Noah obeyed. Soon the flood waters came. But Noah and his family were saved! Again, Noah praised the Lord!

You can read
the whole story
in Genesis,
chapters 6 to 9!

3

If you have breath, you are alive.

And if you are alive, you should give thanks

to the Lord for all He has done.

You should praise Him, for life is the

most important gift God has given to you.

Share the gift. Tell others about God's love.

And as long as you have breath, praise the Lord.

for me today!

let's sing!

Let Everything That Has Breath

Let everything, everything that has breath,
Let everything, everything that has breath,
Praise the Lord, praise the Lord I say!
Can you hear me today?
Come on every girl and boy,
Make a mighty noise and praise the Lord!

Let everything, everything that has breath,
Let everything, everything that has breath,
Praise the Lord, praise the Lord with me!
'Til all the world can see,
He is a great and mighty God.
So where e'er your feet may trod, praise the Lord!

To Live like Jesus...
Have a Positive Attitude

"Do to others what you would have them do to you."
Matthew 7:12

It takes real courage to be nice.

If you were the only person living on the

planet, you wouldn't have to worry about being nice.

There would be no one to disagree with you.

You wouldn't have to be patient. You wouldn't have

to share with anyone. But look around.

There are 6 billion people on this planet. So, how do we

keep a positive attitude in a sometimes negative world?

The best way to do that is to treat others the way

you want to be treated.

Joseph and His Brothers

(Around 1900 B.C.)

Joseph's older brothers did not treat him the way *they* wanted to be treated. They were jealous of Joseph and decided to do a terrible thing. They sold him to an Egyptian merchant who took him to Egypt. But through it all, Joseph kept a positive attitude because he knew God was on his side. Years later, when a famine came to Israel, Joseph's brothers went to Egypt to buy food. Guess who was in charge of the food? That's right: Joseph! But he did not return their unkindness. God's promises helped him keep a positive attitude in spite of what his brothers had done.

You can read the whole story in Genesis, chapters 37 to 45!

Treating others the way you would like
to be treated is called "The Golden Rule."
It is golden because of its great value.
It creates a world where people of all
races and nationalities can live
positive lives together. It's also golden because those
who follow the rule will shine like gold.
Starting today, try to treat others just like you
want them to treat you!

Do to Others

Chorus
Do, do to others what you
Would have them do to you, to you.
Do, do to others what you
Would have them do to you, to you.

(Repeat chorus)

It's gonna take courage to make
This world better, this world better.
If you wanna be nicely treated, hear me.
Be nice, be nice to everyone else.

It's gonna take a hero to make
This world better, this world better.
But you, you can be a hero, you see.
Be nice, be nice if you wanna be treated nice.

If anything is excellent or praiseworthy— think about such things.

Philippians 4:8

THINKIN' 2day

Mrs. Johnson had an excellent class,

twenty of the most well-mannered kids you'd ever find.

She set the standard very high. She expected

excellence in all of their subjects, and she

expected excellence in their behavior.

When they met her standard,

they were excellent! She understood

that good behavior begins with good thinking.

So they always read good books about good people!

Moses Receives the Ten Commandments

(Around 1445 B.C.)

Bible Story

God listed His standards for excellence in the Ten Commandments. When Moses received the Ten Commandments, they were, and still are, God's standard of excellent behavior for every boy and girl. Therefore we should think about them often. Because they teach us how to treat others and how to honor God. They also help us see why we need a Savior. Yes, the Ten Commandments teach us how to live a good life. So, think about them every day!

You can read this story in Exodus, chapter 20!

A steering wheel controls a car.

But what controls the mind?

What you put into it! If something

is excellent in God's eyes, you should think

about it. If something is worthy of praise,

you should think about it. But there are Web sites,

television shows, movies, and magazines that are not

excellent or praiseworthy in God's sight.

Don't give them a second thought!

Seek God's kind of excellence!

for me today!

let's sing!

If Anything Is Excellent

Chorus
Do, do, do, do, do, do, do, do, do, do, do, do!
If anything is excellent,
If anything is praiseworthy,
If anything is excellent or praiseworthy,
Think about such things!

Think about His love, His grace,
That wonderful place we all call heaven,
Seven days a week!
Think about His love, His joy,
Every girl and boy
Think about His love every day! Hear me say,
Think about His love every day, every day!

(Repeat chorus)

To Live like Jesus... Show Kindness

Always try to be kind to each other and to everyone else.

1 Thessalonians 5:15

It was Marcia's first day at school. She had moved from Costa Rica and spoke very little English. She was nervous and quite shy. As class ended, Marcia stood alone. One girl walked over and said, "Hi, Marcia. My name is Wendy. Welcome to our school!" Marcia's face lit up with a bright, beautiful smile.

"Thank you," she answered. Marcia and Wendy began to talk, and before long, Marcia had invited Wendy over to swim in her pool!

Ruth and Naomi

(Between 1210 and 1050 B.C.)

Ruth and her mother-in-law, Naomi, lived together in a place far from Naomi's home. Both Naomi's and Ruth's husbands had died. One day, Naomi decided that it was time to return to her homeland.

But Ruth loved Naomi and did not want her to go alone. Ruth knew exactly what to do. She told Naomi, "Every place you go, I will go" (Ruth 1:16 ICB). Ruth left her home and traveled many miles to Judah to be with Naomi. God soon blessed Ruth for her kindness to Naomi. There Ruth met a man named Boaz, and they were married.

You can read the whole story in the Book of Ruth!

15

Sometimes God whispers to your heart,

"Say a kind word to the visitor,"

or "Go visit the elderly lady across

the street." Being kind is a choice we make.

It is also one of the fruits of the Spirit

mentioned in the Bible. When you pray,

ask God to give you a spirit of kindness.

Then treat it like peanut butter: spread it around!

for me today!

let's sing!

Try to Be Kind

Sometimes God is calling you, child.
Sometimes He's got a job to do.
One of His children may be in despair,
And a little kindness you could surely share.

Chorus
Always, always try to be kind.
Always, always try to be kind,
To each other, sister and brother,
To everyone, to everyone else,
Be kind.

Sometimes we don't want to listen.
Sometimes when God is calling us,
But one of His children's waiting there.
Maybe one day you might need some kindness, too.

Show proper respect to everyone.

1 Peter 2:17

"Lightning can be a very dangerous thing," said Mr. Butler. Mr. Butler was a meteorologist. But we call him the weather man. He had come to visit our school. "Lightning is a very powerful bolt of electricity," he explained. "It can strike trees and even people. Hundreds of people each year die because they do not use caution during lightning storms." Yes, lightning is very, very powerful, but did you know that prayer is very powerful too?

David and Goliath

(Around 1025 B.C.)

Bible
Story

Goliath was a very big and powerful man.
But he had a lesson to learn about the power of prayer.
Goliath was a Philistine warrior.
He stood over nine feet tall! One day, Israel met the
Philistine army for battle. Each morning,
for 40 days, Goliath would stand in the valley and
shout insults at Israel and their God. Goliath was
about to find out how powerful prayer really is!

When David heard Goliath mocking God, he marched out
to do battle. Although David was little, he prayed big
prayers! David carried a slingshot with him and said,
"I come against you in the name of the LORD"
(1 Samuel 17:45). Hurling a stone at Goliath, *Bam!*
David hit him squarely in the head. Down went the
giant! Goliath was no match for a mighty prayer
and a mighty God!

You can read this story in 1 Samuel, chapter 17!

Be sure to show proper respect for everyone you meet. All people were created by God, made in His image. And for that, they deserve your respect.

You should never disrespect others because of the way they look, the language they speak, or the things they have. If we respect others, they will respect us too! Peter said to show R-E-S-P-E-C-T to everyone!

for me today!

let's sing!

Show Proper Respect

Chorus
Show proper respect to everyone you meet,
Kids across the street, around the block.
It doesn't stop there.
Show proper respect to everyone you meet—
Big or small, short or tall, doesn't matter at all!
Show proper respect!

R-E-S-P-E-C-T!
We can spell it,
But do we know what it means?
R-E-S-P-E-C-T!
They can tell it
When they see it in you and me.

R-E-S-P-E-C-T!   (Repeat chorus)
We can sing it,
But do we give it away?
R-E-S-P-E-C-T!
When you bring it to the world,
They all shout hooray!

(Repeat chorus)

To Live like Jesus... Be a Friend

A FRIEND loves at all times.

Proverbs 17:17

THINKIN' 2day

There's nothing better than having a good friend you can count on—someone who's always there in good times and bad. Someone you can talk to and someone who'll listen.  That's the kind of friend you should try to be to others. "Fair-weather" friends seem to disappear when things get tough. But a real friend is always

 there to give a smile, to listen, and to help!

Jonathan and David Were Friends

(Around 1010 B.C.)

Jonathan and David were best friends.

Jonathan's father was the king of Israel,

so David and Jonathan stayed in the palace.

They enjoyed being together. They respected each

other. Jonathan gave David his robe and tunic,

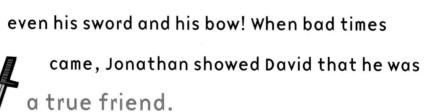 even his sword and his bow! When bad times

came, Jonathan showed David that he was

a true friend.

Real friendship is based on love and a giving spirit. Jonathan had a giving spirit. You, too, can show your friendship by giving of your time, your abilities, and even sharing your things to help others. A friend loves at all times: the good times, the bad times . . . any time. And that's what true friendship is all about!

for me today!

let's sing!

A Friend Loves at All Times!

Oh, a friend loves at all times!
Oh, a friend loves at all times!
Morning, noon, or night,
A friend is a delight,
For a friend loves at all times!

Oh, a friend loves at all times!
Oh, a friend loves at all times!
When evening shadows fall,
A friend will come to call,
For a friend loves at all times!

Oh, a friend loves at all times!
Oh, a friend loves at all times!
When stars do shine above,
A friend will speak in love,
For a friend loves at all times!

24

To Live like Jesus... Remember GoD

REMEMBER your Creator in the days of your youth.

Ecclesiastes 12:1

THINKIN' 2day

Erin can be so forgetful sometimes. The other day, she had a flat tire on her bicycle. No problem! She knew how to fix it. She was almost finished when Mom called for lunch. After lunch, she went back down to the garage and hopped on her bike. Off she went, but suddenly, the front wheel started wobbling. It came completely off the bicycle! She had forgotten something very important: she had not tighten the nuts that hold the tire in place!

Josiah, the Young King

(Around 622 B.C.)

Josiah's father was the king of Israel.
But he had forgotten something very important.
He had forgotten about the Lord and
worshiped idols instead. Josiah became king
when he was only eight years old. He destroyed the
idols and sent workers to repair the temple of the Lord.

Then the Book of the Law was found, covered with
dust. The book was read to the young king.
Upon hearing the Word, he knew his people
had sinned. Josiah asked God for forgiveness.

Josiah promised the Lord he would always
remember Him.

Memory is really a cool thing.
It helps you to make the right choices.
It helps you to live your life with
fewer difficulties. If you remember
God's Word, you can act upon it and live
a good life. If you forget about God, it can bring
terrible trouble. In all that you do, remember the Lord,
your Creator, and His commands.
Don't forget to remember the Creator this week!

for me today!

let's sing!

Remember Your Creator

Remember your Creator in the days of your youth!
Remember your Creator in the days of your youth!
Remember your Creator in the days of your youth,
And you will live a happy life! Amen!
Don't forget, don't forget,
To remember the Lord and His promises!
Don't forget, don't forget,
To remember the Lord and His promises!

(Repeat)

To Live like Jesus...
Speak No Unwholesome Talk

Do not let any Unwholesome talk come out of your mouths, but only what is helpful for building others up.

Ephesians 4:29

The football stadium was packed. Spirits were high, and the team had played their hearts out. It was tied, 31 to 31, with three seconds left on the clock. The ball was snapped. The kick went up. "No good!" shouted the referee. In the stands behind Marcus and his dad, they heard a young man yelling a lot of really bad words! Dad turned to the young man and said, "Your bad words won't affect the score, but they do affect

others around you!"

29

Job Faces Many Trials

(Around 2000 B.C.)

Job faced many trials, yet no unwholesome talk came out of his mouth. Satan was allowed to take his ten children. But Job didn't sin in what he said. Satan was allowed to take all of Job's possessions. But Job didn't sin in what he said. Satan was allowed to make Job sick. Even when Job's wife told him to curse God and die, he didn't sin. In all of his troubles, Job did not speak unkind words to God.

Your tongue is like a rudder on a ship—small with a big purpose—and it must be controlled. It must not speak words that are unwholesome.

Those words may hinder others from seeing Jesus. Always speak good words that encourage, no matter what happens. Speaking bad words won't change anything. But a good word, spoken at just the right time, can change everything!

for me today!

let's sing!

Unwholesome Talk

Chorus
Do not, do-do-do not
Do-do-do not let any, let any,
Do not, do-do-do not
Do-do-do not let any, let any,
Do not, do-do-do not,
Do-do-do not let any, let any,
Unwholesome talk
Come out of your ma-ma-ma mouth!
Ma-ma-ma mouth!
But only what
Only what
Only what is helpful for
Building others uppity, uppity, uppity, uppity!
But only what
Only what
Only what is helpful for
Building others uppity, uppity, uppity, uppity!

My mouth will declare your praise.

Psalm 51:15

So many **different** kinds of words can come out of your mouth. You can speak a word of kindness. You can say thank you. You can use words to comfort someone in need. You can even shout an alarm: "Help!"

Your words can really make a difference in the lives of others.

Solomon Was a Wise Man

(Solomon reigned from 970 to 930 B.C.)

Solomon was the wisest man ever to live.

He knew a lot of words. He used his words to write

over one thousand songs to the Lord.

He also wrote three thousand proverbs.

What a difference his words made! He used them to

declare the praise of the Lord, just like his father David.

It was Solomon who wrote:

"Saying the right word at the right time is so pleasing!"

(Proverbs 15:23 ICB). His mouth and his words declared

God's praise!

You can read the wise words of Solomon in the Book of Proverbs!

35

How will people know that your God is a wonderful God unless you tell them? You have to show them with your actions and tell them the story of God. Sure, you believe in the Lord on the inside. But you have to start believing out loud. You can make every day a show-and-tell day. Show and tell them about God's love!

for me today!

let's sing!

Declare Your Praise

My mouth will declare Your praises, Oh Lord!
My mouth will declare Your praises, Oh Lord!
I praise You for the morning sun,
Praise You for the day,
Praise You for the evening sky,
Oh Lord, I have to say...

My mouth will declare Your praises, Oh Lord!
My mouth will declare Your praises, Oh Lord!
I praise You for the moon at night,
Praise You for the stars,
Praise You Lord for all You've done,
Praise You for who You are!

To Live like Jesus...
Keep GoD's Commands

"KEEP my commands and you will live."
Proverbs 4:4

THINKIN' 2day

The rain was pouring down.

The wipers could barely clear the windshield.

Thunder crashed and lightning filled the sky.

It was only a few more miles to the bridge.

Suddenly, Juan saw a very bright light up ahead.

A policeman with a flare was standing in the downpour.

"The bridge is out!" he shouted. "Go back!"

Juan's dad thanked the policeman.

His warning had saved their lives.

37

Jeremiah Reminds Israel

(Around 587 B.C.)

The prophet Jeremiah warned Israel to never ignore God's warnings. The nation of Israel had served and obeyed God for many years. But as time passed, the people forgot about God's commands. They began to sin more and more. Soon, an enemy of Israel came and made them their slaves. Jeremiah wept for the nation of Israel. But he reminded them that even though they had forgotten God,

God had not forgotten them.

God's commandments show you the
way and serve as a warning.
They are like light in a very dark world.
They show you the right way to live your life.
They are also a warning, telling you, "There's danger ahead!
Don't go that way!" Every day you must choose to obey or
ignore God's commands. If you obey His commands,
you will live an exciting life!

for me today!

let's sing!

Keep My Commands

Chorus
Keep My commandments and you will live.
Keep My commandments and you will live.
If you keep My commandments,
You will live.
If you keep My commandments,
You will live; you will live.

God's Word is like a flare in the darkest night,
Showing us the way.
God's Word is like a flare shining forth its light,
Helping us to see where we ought to be.

(Repeat chorus)

God's Word is wonderful, keeping us from harm,
Showing us the way.
God's Word is wonderful; it sounds a big alarm,
When sin I do see there in front of me.

(Repeat chorus)

Seek first his kingdom and his righteousness, and all these things will be given to you.

Matthew 6:33

THINKIN'
2day

The End

The Cinema Plaza was fantastic!

There were 20 movies playing in different theatres, all at the same time. "Enjoy *Cartoon Town*. I'll be back at 8:30," Cara's mom called as she watched Cara and Allison walk into the theatre. As the girls passed a movie poster, Allison said, "Hey, Cara, let's go see the scary movie instead. No one will know." Cara knew her mom trusted her to do what's right, and she didn't want to let her down. "Nah, *Cartoon Town* is just fine with me," Cara replied, and she stepped up to the ticket booth.

tickets

Shadrach, Meshach, and Abednego

(Around 580 B.C.)

Shadrach, Meshach, and Abednego

knew that God trusted them to do what was right.

So when the king set up a statue and told all his

governors to worship it, Shadrach, Meshach, and

Abednego refused. They knew that one day they

would answer to God, who was greater than any king.

The king ordered them to be thrown into a fiery

furnace. They told the king, "God . . . is able to save

us . . . But even if he does not, . . . we will not serve

your gods" (Daniel 3:17–18). Into the fire they went.

But they were not burned. They didn't even smell like

smoke. God saved them because they obeyed Him!

You can read the whole story in Daniel, chapter 3!

Cara had been trusted to do the right thing. She knew that if she disobeyed her mother, her mother would no longer trust her. She would answer to her mother, not her friend. That's how it is when we're tempted to disobey the Lord. Who will you answer to? The friends who are tempting you or the Lord? That's right! Just remember, seek His righteousness first!

for me today!

let's sing!

Seek First His Kingdom

Seek first His kingdom
And His righteousness.
Seek first His kingdom
And all these things will be given to you,
All these things will be given to you.

Joy will be given to you.
Peace will be given to you.
Love will be given to you,
If we will seek the kingdom of God!
If we will seek the kingdom of God!

(Repeat)

Children, Obey your parents in the Lord.

Ephesians 6:1

Tasha didn't always obey the first time she was told to do something. Many times, her mother would have to ask two or three times before she would obey. One day she and her mother were kicking a soccer ball in the front yard. With one kick, it rolled into the street. Without paying attention to the passing car, Tasha ran into the street. "Tasha, stop!" her mother shouted. *Honk! Screech!* The car barely missed hitting her! Learning to obey the first time is a very good habit.

Jonah and the Whale

(Around 785 B.C.)

Poor Jonah had to learn to obey the hard way.
God told Jonah to go to Nineveh and preach.

Jonah didn't want to, so he sailed the other way.
God sent a terrible storm which tossed the big
ship up and down. Jonah knew the storm was his fault.
He told the sailors, "Throw me into the sea . . . and it will
become calm" (Jonah 1:12). Jonah was tossed overboard
and . . . *GULP!* He was swallowed by a great, big fish.

For three days, Jonah was inside the belly of that fish
as it swam through the ocean. He promised God, "I will
obey this time." The fish spit him out on dry land.
Jonah **finally obeyed** and went to Nineveh!

You can read the whole story in the Book of Jonah!

47

for me today!

Tasha was almost hurt because she did not obey her mother the first time.

Jonah spent three very unpleasant days inside a big fish because he did not obey his heavenly Father the first time. Learning to obey your parents is a very important sign of growing up.

Your parents have wisdom, and God has said in His Word that you should obey your parents. God has *all* wisdom so you should trust and obey Him—the first time!

let's sing!

Children, Obey Your Parents

Children, obey your parents in the Lord,
For this is right.
Children, obey your parents in the Lord,
For this is right.
Honor your father and mother,
Which is the first commandment with a promise
That it may go well with you
And that you may enjoy long life on the earth!

(Repeat)

To Live like Jesus...
Listen

MY MEMORY **verse**

Everyone should be quick to **listen**, slow to speak and slow to become angry.
James 1:19

THINKIN' **2day**

Ryan was always talking in class.

As Mr. Myers was passing out the tests, Ryan just kept on talking. Mr. Myers said, "Listen carefully. First, read every question, and then begin the test."

Everyone did as Mr. Myers said—everyone except for Ryan. He wasn't listening. Within minutes, everyone began to leave the classroom. Ryan wondered how they could possibly be finished! But then, as he got to the last question, he read, "Now go back and only answer question number one."

49

The Parable of the Sower

(Around A.D. 28)

Jesus said, "Listen!" He had something very important to say. He told the story of a farmer who went out to sow some seed. Some seeds fell on the path and birds ate it. Some fell on the rocks and were scorched by the sun. Some fell in thorn bushes and were choked. But some fell on good soil and produced a crop. Jesus explained, "The seed is the word of God" (Luke 8:11). Some people are like seeds on the path. They hear the Word of God, but Satan comes and takes it away. Some are like seeds on the rocks. They receive the Word but fall away when trials come. Some are like seed sown among thorns. The Word is choked out by worry. But others listen and obey. They receive God's blessings!

50

You can read
this story
in Luke, chapter 8!

Seeds

It's easier to open your ears if your mouth is closed. When you listen, you can learn. But with so many voices calling out in this world, who should you listen to? The voice of God, of course! He speaks through the Bible. So today, be quick to listen and be slow to speak!  for me today!

let's sing!

Everyone Should Be Quick to Listen

Chorus
Everyone should be quick to listen.
Everyone should be quick to listen,
Slow to speak and slow to become angry.
Everyone should be quick to listen.
Everyone should be quick to listen,
Slow to speak and that's how it oughta' be!

It's easier to open your ears
If your mouth is closed.
But some are breezier than a hurricane
That blows and blows and blows!

(Repeat chorus)

It's sensible to listen and learn,
So listen now to me!
It's reprehensible—what?—I'll make it clear.
Button those lips and brighter you'll be!

(Repeat chorus)

52

"Give, and it will be given to you."

Luke 6:38

Keisha looked at the offering plate. It was coming her way. She reached in her purse and pulled out a quarter. She wanted to give more than that! The plate was full of dollars, checks, and envelopes stuffed with money. She just had twenty-five cents, but she gave it all. Keisha wondered,

What can God do with my little offering?

Jesus Feeds Thousands

(Around A.D. 29)

Jesus once made a LOT from a little offering.

He was preaching on a hillside to five thousand people.

When evening came, the people were very hungry.

But there was no food. One boy offered his lunch of five

barley loaves and two small fish to Jesus.

But how far would that go to feed so many?

Jesus blessed the loaves and fish. Then five thousand

people ate dinner and had as much as they wanted.

It was a great miracle!

You can read the whole story in John, chapter 6!

A little in God's hands is better than

for me today!

a lot in your own hands.
He has promised in the Bible that if you
are willing to give unselfishly to others,
He is willing to give back to you an
even greater blessing. Imagine a blessing so big
that your house wouldn't be able to hold it. It's nice to know
that you can never "outgive" God! Be a happy giver!

let's sing!

Give

Chorus
Jesus said:
Give and it will be given unto you.
Jesus said:
Give and it will be given unto you.

We must understand
That a little in God's hand
Is truly better than
A lot in our own.
We must understand
There's a blessing from His hand
If we give a hungry man
What he needs—this we believe!

(Repeat chorus)

We must understand,
Oh, that giving is God's plan,
And all across our land
Lift our voice and sing.
People understand
That a selfish heart is bland,
But a giving heart is grand.
So let's give, and learn to live!

Forgive as the Lord forgave you.
Colossians 3:13b

It is important to always to treat others with kindness.

That seems like an easy thing to do, right?

Well, it is easy until someone is mean to *you*.

That's when you have to make a choice. Do you return

meanness for meanness? Do you hold a grudge?

No! There's a better choice.

You can learn to forgive!

Peter Learns to Forgive

(Around A.D. 29)

Bible Story

Peter once came to Jesus.

He wanted to learn to forgive. So he asked Jesus,

"How many times shall I forgive my brother when he

sins against me? Up to seven times?" (Matthew 18:21).

Jesus told Peter that he should forgive more than

seven times. He should forgive seven times seventy!

Jesus explained that there was no limit to God's

forgiveness, so Peter should have no limit to his

forgiveness toward others.

You can read
the whole story
in Matthew, chapter 18!

If there is ever a time that someone treats you unfairly, learn the lesson Peter learned from Jesus. Forgive that person as the Lord forgave you. Think about the many times you have been forgiven by your heavenly Father.

Then choose to act like Jesus. Forgive!

for me today!

let's sing!

Forgive

We learn to live when we forgive,
Just the way that Jesus did.
We learn to love like God above,
When we can love the ones who shove.
It's not an easy thing to do, child,
But now we have a song for you, child,
Saying to the world, every boy and girl!

Chorus
Forgive a little bit, gonna be like Jesus!
Forgive a little bit, gonna be like Him!
Forgive a little bit, never gonna quit livin' for Him!
Forgive a little bit, as the Lord forgave you!
Forgive a little bit, gonna be like Him!
We learn to live when we forgive,
We forgive. Again and again.

We learn to care when we forbear
Unkind words, a call unfair.
We learn to grow, God's love we show,
When we forgive and let it go.
It's not an easy thing to do, child,
But now we have a song for you, child,
Saying to the world, every boy and girl!

(Repeat chorus)

60

"Be merciful, just as your Father is merciful."

Luke 6:36

Brittany had worked so hard on her homework assignment. *How could she have left for school without it?* It was due today, and it counted as half her grade. She was nearly in tears when she walked up to her teacher's desk. "Mr. Rhymer, I'm sorry, but I forgot my homework. I really did it, and I worked so hard." Mr. Rhymer forgave her and said, "You've been a wonderful student, Brittany. Could you bring it tomorrow?"

61

The Unmerciful Servant

(Around A.D. 28)

Jesus spoke of a servant who asked for mercy. He owed the king a lot of money. But he could not pay the debt. The servant begged for mercy. "Be patient . . . and I will pay back everything" (Matthew 18:26).

The king showed great mercy and forgave the servant's debt. But that same servant found another man who owed him money. He, too, begged for mercy. But no mercy was shown. The servant had the man who was in debt to him thrown into prison. When the king heard what the evil servant had done, he was very angry.

You can read this story in Matthew, chapter 18!

Justice is getting what you deserve.

Mercy is getting something good

that you do *not* deserve. We can learn

to show mercy by doing the thing Jesus did.

He had mercy upon the sick, the dying, even *you*.

Everyone who sins deserves death. But because of Jesus,

you are given mercy. Sometimes, the thing you don't deserve is

the thing you need the most!

Be Merciful

Chorus
Be merciful, be merciful, be merciful,
Just as your Father is merciful.
Be merciful, be merciful, be merciful,
Just as your Father is merciful.

Mercy me, Lord! I hope You'll be, Lord,
Merciful to me.
Mercy me, Lord!
I do believe, Lord,
Mercy and grace we all do need.

(Repeat chorus)

Mercy me, Lord! How can it be, Lord?
You're merciful to me.
Mercy me, Lord! Together we, Lord,
Praise You for mercy!
And it's how we wanna be.

(Repeat chorus)

A GENTLE answer turns away wrath.

Proverbs 15:1

THINKIN' 2day

People can have different

views on the same subject. Some like the rain;

some do not. Some like it cold; some like it hot.

Sometimes differences can cause tempers to flare.

If you're not careful, your disagreement can turn into

an argument. In those times, you should be

very careful with your words. It is more

difficult to settle a disagreement when

someone is angry.

Jesus Gave a Gentle Answer

(Around A.D. 29)

The religious leaders and teachers brought a woman to Jesus. She had broken the law. These leaders had angry hearts. They thought she should be killed with stones.

They asked Jesus if He thought they were doing the right thing. But Jesus answered, "If any one of you is without sin, let him be the first to throw a stone" (John 8:7). Suddenly, it got very quiet. They all walked away ashamed. Jesus' gentle answer turned them away and saved the young woman.

You can read this story in John, chapter 8!

Sometimes, you may have disagreements with others. Even friends and family may get very angry. If this happens, it is always best to do what Jesus did. He spoke a gentle answer. Shouting unkind words at each other won't help you settle your argument. Be like Jesus. Speak a gentle word.

for me today!

let's sing!

A Gentle Answer

Chorus
A gentle answer turns away the wrath
Of those who come your way. I say,
A gentle answer calms the voice,
Stills the heart; it's heaven's choice.

A gentle word, a voice so kind
Can move a heart, change a mind.
A gentle word, a voice of love
Calms a spirit with joy because

(Repeat chorus)

A gentle voice, a word of peace,
Can calm the soul, make wars cease.
A gentle voice, a glad refrain
Like a medicine that soothes the pain.

(Repeat chorus)

To Live like Jesus...
Love Others

MY MEMORY
verse

"Love your neighbor as yourself."

Matthew 19:19

THINKIN'
2 day

Rosa had never seen snow falling the way it did

on that day. She tried to catch snowflakes on her

tongue as she walked with her dad toward the mall.

As they made their last turn, Rosa saw a homeless man

huddled on the sidewalk. He had no coat. Without

saying a word, her father took off his coat and covered

the man. Then he said, "I'll pay for your room tonight

at that motel," pointing across the street.

Rosa has never forgotten that moment.

69

The Good Samaritan

(Around A.D. 28)

Jesus once told a parable about a man traveling from Jerusalem to Jericho. The man was robbed, beaten, and left lying on the side of the road. A passing priest saw the man, but did nothing to help him. Next, another helper from the church passed by, but he, too, did nothing. Then came a Samaritan. He stopped and cared for the man. He bandaged his wounds and took him to an inn and even paid for the room himself.

After Jesus told the story, He asked, "Which of these three do you think was a neighbor . . . ?" (Luke 10:36). Surely it was the one who met the needs of the hurting!

So, who is *your* neighbor?

Your neighbor is anyone who has a need that you can meet. You don't have to look very hard to find people with needs in the world. Perhaps in your own family, school, or church, you know someone who could use a visit or a cheerful word.

Just think: if you love your neighbor as yourself, God can change the entire neighborhood!

for me today!

let's sing!

Love Your Neighbor

Chorus
Love your neighbor.
Love your neighbor as yourself.
Love your neighbor.
Love your neighbor as yourself.
Who is my neighbor?
Anyone who has a need!
So just love your neighbor,
And that's the way it's s'posed to be.

We don't have to look too far.
Love your neighbor.
Find a need wherever we are.
Love your neighbor.
Speak a word; lend a hand.
Love your neighbor, understand.
Here's a chance to be a friend
Let a better day begin.

(Repeat chorus)

Someone in your school today,
Love your neighbor
Is feelin' down and so I say,
Love your neighbor
Speak a word; lend a hand
Love your neighbor, understand.
Here's a chance to be a friend.
Let a better day begin.

(Repeat chorus)

To Live like Jesus... Have Patience

Be patient, bearing with one another in love.

Ephesians 4:2

THINKIN' 2day

Matt really didn't mean to do it.

He had one hand on the glass, one hand on the door.

But when Sparky barked and came bounding through

the door—*splash!*—milk went everywhere. Mom grabbed a

handful of paper towels and said patiently,

"It's just a little spill. It's okay."

Together Mom and Matt cleaned up the milk.

The Prodigal Son

(Around A.D. 28)

Jesus tells of a patient father who loved his two sons dearly. The younger one said, "Give me my share of the family inheritance now. I am leaving for a far country." The loving father did as his son had asked. The son moved away and soon wasted all of his money. He became so hungry that he took a job feeding pigs and even ate their food. One day, he came to his senses. *I'll go home and work for my father,* he thought. When he was almost home, his patient father ran to him and hugged him. The boy said, "I am no longer worthy to be called your son. May I work for you?" But his father loved him and celebrated his return!

You can read
this story in
Luke, chapter 15!

A big part of loving someone is showing patience. Sometimes, you have to put up with things you don't like. No one plants a seed of corn in the ground and comes back the next day asking, "Where's the corn?" You must be patient. Good things take a little time. Today, practice a little patience with your family and friends.

for me today!

let's sing!

Be Patient

You've planted a seed in a garden today.
Be patient, for this we do know.
You've planted a seed,
Now there's coming a day.
Be patient, the flower will grow.

Chorus
Be patient, be patient,
Bearing with one another in love.
Be patient, be patient,
Be patient, the flower will grow.

You've planted a seed in the Lord's holy name.
Be patient for this we do know.
You've planted a seed.
Pray in time for the rain.
Be patient, the flower will grow.

(Repeat chorus)

To Live like Jesus...
Love God

MY MEMORY
verse

THINKIN'
2day

Love the LORD your God with all your heart and with all your soul and with all your strength.

Deuteronomy 6:5

Twenty anxious girls sat down on the gym floor. Coach Maxwell came into the room and spoke. "If you are going to play basketball for the Thunder Cats, I will be here every evening, Monday through Friday, from 4:00 to 7:00. You will need to be here every day for practice." Emily's hand slowly went up into the air. "I have piano lessons on Tuesdays at 5:00. May I be excused for that?" The coach answered, "Absolutely not!" Emily loved playing the piano more than she loved basketball. She would not be able to try out for basketball. She could not give her all to the team.

The Rich, Young Ruler

(Around A.D. 30)

A rich, young man once came to Jesus.

He asked what he must do to have eternal life.

Jesus said that he must keep *all* the commandments.

The young man said that he had kept all the

commandments. Then Jesus said that he

should sell *all* he owned and give to the poor.

But the young man could not do this because he loved

the things he owned more than he loved the Lord.

He didn't love God with *all* of his heart.

You can read this story in Mark, chapter 10!

God wants you to love Him with your whole heart. If you are half-hearted in your love for Him, you may be saving the other half for the things of this world. Nothing in this world should keep you from heaven. Today, love God with *all* your heart and see the difference!

for me today!

let's sing!

With All Your Heart

God wants us to really love Him,
Love Him with all our hearts,
Night or day, work or play.
If you travel far away,
It doesn't matter wherever you are.
You know that God wants us to really love Him,
Love Him with all our hearts.
The Bible says,
Love the Lord with all your heart
And with all your soul
And with all your strength.

God wants us to really love Him,
Love Him with all our hearts.
Stay awhile; pray awhile.
Tell Him 'bout your day awhile,
It doesn't matter wherever you are,
You know that God wants us to really love Him,
Love Him with all our hearts.
The Bible says,
Love the Lord with all your heart
And with all your soul
And with all your strength.

"Whoever can be trusted with very little can also be trusted with much."

Luke 16:10

"Mr. President, what was your very first public office?" asked the fifth grader.

The president was visiting a middle school in Nashville, Tennessee. "Now, that's a very good question," responded the president. "My very first public office was held at Dunbar Elementary School, where I was elected treasurer of Mrs. Casto's sixth-grade class. The other students trusted me to collect and turn in the lunch money each day."

The Parable of the Talents

Bible Story

A master once trusted his servants with his money. To one, he gave five thousand dollars. To another, he gave two thousand, and to another, he gave one thousand. Then the master went on a long journey. When he returned, he called the three servants in for a report. The one with five thousand had gained five thousand more. The one with two thousand had gained two thousand more.

"Well done . . . ," said the master. "You have been faithful with a few things; I will put you in charge of many things" (Matthew 25:21). But the man with one thousand dollars had gained nothing.

He could not be trusted again!

To get a big job with big responsibility, you must first show that you can be trusted to do little jobs. The president didn't start by managing a whole country. He started with a small job in the sixth grade.

for me today!

Trust is something you earn every day. If you are faithful to complete the little jobs around the house, then you show everyone you are ready for bigger and more important jobs. Doing a little job well can lead to BIG things!

let's sing!

Whoever Can Be Trusted

Whoever, whoever, whoever,
Whoever can be trusted,
Whoever, whoever, whoever,
Whoever can be trusted,
With very little
I know it's true!
Can also be trusted with much
Can you?
Whoever, whoever, whoever,
Whoever can be trusted...
You want a big job.
You want a big job.
So do the little job right
To show you're in the know!
You're responsible!

(Repeat)

Don't let anyone look down on you because you are young, but set an example for the believers in speech, in life, in love, in faith and in purity.

1 Timothy 4:12

Celebrities can have a great influence on many people. They set examples that many will follow. If they are polite and you see that example, perhaps you will be polite. If they wear their hair a

certain way or dress a certain way, a lot of people will follow. You, too, can influence the people around you with your actions. And others can learn from your example.

Paul, a Good Example

(Around A.D. 55)

Bible Story

Paul wrote a letter to the church at Corinth. In it, he makes a remarkable statement. It is one that few of us would dare make. He said, "Follow my example, as I follow the example of Christ" (1 Corinthians 11:1). Paul was learning and obeying the teachings of Jesus and living them out in his daily life. His speech, love, and faith showed the world that he was a Christian!

87

Is your life a good example of the Christian life? As a believer, you need to set a good example. Your speech needs to be clean and pure. Your life needs to be free from sinful habits. And your faith should be growing. Even though you are young, you can set a good example for others. You're never too young to be a good example!

let's sing!

Because You Are Young

Don't let anyone
Don't let anyone
Look down on you.
Don't let anyone
Don't let anyone
Look down on you
Because, because, because you are young.
No! Don't let anyone
Don't let anyone
Look down on you.
Set an example for believers in life.
Set an example for believers in love.
Set an example for believers in faith.
And don't let anyone,
No, not anyone, look down on you.

To Live like Jesus...
Have Joy

"The JOY of the LORD is your strength."

Nehemiah 8:10

THINKIN' 2day

Robert was a member of the Cub Scouts.

There was nothing he wanted more than to earn his Arrow of Light award! So when other kids were playing video games or  watching cartoons, Robert worked hard to reach his goal.

He knew the sacrifice would be worth it when they presented the badge to him at the Pack meeting.

The thought of the joy of that moment kept him going!

89

Paul Lives a Godly Life

(Around A.D. 59-61)

Bible Story

Paul knew how difficult it was to work toward a great reward. When he chose to live a godly life, people made fun of him, and he was even put in jail! But Paul kept going, knowing the reward in the end would be worth it all. And at the end of his struggles, he looked back and said, "I have fought the good fight, I have finished the race, I have kept the faith. Now there is in store for me the crown of righteousness, which the Lord . . . will award to me on that day" (2 Timothy 4:7–8).

When you have a tough job to do,
just thinking about the reward to come
is enough to keep you going!
In your Christian journey, you may face
many trials. But the joy of knowing that God's
servants are bound for heaven will help you through the day,
the year, even the rest of your life.
Yes, the joy of the Lord is your strength to reach the finish line!

for me today!

let's sing!

The Joy of the Lord

Chorus
I've got the joy, joy, joy down in my heart!
I've got the joy, joy, joy down in my heart
The joy of the Lord is my strength!
Yes, indeed!
The joy of the Lord is my strength!
Say it again!
The joy of the Lord is my strength!
Yes, indeed!
The joy of the Lord is my strength!

When trouble comes my way, Lord,
All I have to say, Lord,
The joy of the Lord is my strength
'Cause I know my Lord is there
To fight my battles anywhere!

(Repeat chorus)

When sadness fills my day, Lord,
Bad news comes my way, Lord,
The joy of the Lord is my strength!
'Cause I know my Lord is there
To fight my battles anywhere!

(Repeat chorus)

92